# DAMS

## MAN-MADE WONDERS

Jason Cooper

Rourke Enterprises, Inc.
Vero Beach, Florida 32964

PHOTO CREDITS

© Frank S. Balthis: cover, pages 8, 15, 18;
© Lynn M. Stone: title page, pages 7, 10, 12;
© James P. Rowan: pages 4, 13; © William H. Mullins: pages 17, 21

**LIBRARY OF CONGRESS**
**Library of Congress Cataloging-in-Publication Data**
Cooper, Jason, 1942-
    Dams / by Jason Cooper.
    p.   cm. — (Man made wonders)
    Includes index.
    Summary:   Describes the construction, purpose, and parts of
dams throughout the world.
    ISBN 0-86592-627-1
    1. Dams—Juvenile literature.   [1. Dams.]
I. Title.   II. Series.
TC540.C66   1991
627'.8—dc20                          91-12313
                                       CIP
                                       AC

# TABLE OF CONTENTS

## DAMS

Beavers use their paws to build dams of mud and sticks. People use heavy machines to build dams of concrete. But dams built by beavers and people do the same thing. They hold water back. Dams also change water flow, the speed and amount of water that moves forward.

Stopping most of a river's flow, dams make lakes and ponds. Some of those lakes made by people are over 100 miles long.

Dams may be little mounds of soil or huge, concrete **barriers.** Some dams reach nearly the height of the world's tallest buildings.

*Roosevelt Dam in Arizona*

## EARLY DAMS

Beavers built dams long before people did. Even so, the first known dams built by people are very old. They were dams built of brick and stone by people almost 4,500 years ago.

Old dams were built with natural building supplies—rocks, wood, and dirt. They worked, but not nearly as well as modern dams work. High water washed dirt away, and leaks were common.

*Beaver dam in Missouri*

## USES OF DAMS

By keeping water trapped in a lake, dams help prevent floods in some places. Water held by dams is also used to make electricity. Dams can release huge waterfalls. The force of the waterfall is used to power machines that produce electricity. This is known as **hydroelectric** power.

Dams supply water for crops. They store up drinking water and water for boating and fishing, too.

Years ago, dam water turned waterwheels which powered **mills.** Mills ground grain into flour.

*Hydroelectric power station at base of Shasta Dam, California*

# EARTH DAMS

Most dams are made of earth (dirt) or of earth and rocks. They are sometimes called earthen, earth-fill, or earth and rock-fill dams.

**Dikes** are earth dams used to keep rivers and lakes from flooding. Dikes act like tall river banks or shorelines.

If water pours over an earth dam, it can wash soil away. These dams are usually covered by stones or with concrete for protection.

The most common earth dams make farm ponds.

*Connecticut farm pond
formed by earth dam*

*Water wheel at Grau Mill, Oakbrook, Illinois*

*Bollinger Mill and dam at Burfordville, Missouri*

## CONCRETE DAMS

Concrete dams may be hollow or they may be solid concrete. Both types can be supported by steel.

Solid concrete dams are extremely heavy and strong. They can hold back tremendous water pressure.

The Grand Coulee Dam in Washington is the largest concrete dam in North America. The Itaipu Dam in South America is the world's largest concrete dam. It was completed in 1982.

The tallest concrete dam is Switzerland's Grand Dixence Dam.

*Grand Coulee Dam, Washington*

## PARTS OF A DAM

A dam is basically a solid fence. Water rushes against it but cannot pass. The water backs up into a **reservoir,** which is the pond or lake.

A dam cannot hold all the water which streams into its reservoir. Dams are built with openings called outlets. The outlet is usually a pipe or gate that releases water when it is opened.

The **spillway** is an outlet that lets water spill from the dam's upper level.

*Outlets release water from John Day Dam on the Columbia River*

## PROBLEMS WITH DAMS

Dams are not always welcome. The reservoirs they make flood ground that had been dry. People may be forced to leave their homes, and important land features may disappear under the new lake.

Dams may also change the kinds of animals and plants that live in a river or lake. The kinds of fish that live in a river, for instance, may not be able to survive behind a dam.

Dams are expensive to build. Sometimes the benefit of a dam—hydroelectric power, for example—is not worth its cost.

*Arizona's Glen Canyon Dam
flooded beautiful Glen Canyon*

## MAJOR AMERICAN DAMS

In the United States, 85 big dams have been built along the Columbia River and rivers that feed into it.

Hoover Dam on the Colorado River forms giant Lake Mead. In the Southeast, dozens of dams were built along the Tennessee River and its feeder streams in the 1930s. The dams provided flood control and cheap electric power. These dams and lakes are part of the famous TVA—Tennessee Valley Authority—project.

*Bonneville, a major dam on the Columbia River system*

## MAJOR INTERNATIONAL DAMS

The world's highest dams are the Nurek and Rogunsky dams in the Soviet Union. Rogunsky, at 1,066 feet, is the taller of the two.

Egypt's famous Aswan High Dam holds the floodwaters of the Nile River. The dam produces electricity and provides water during the dry season.

Before the Nile River backed up behind the dam, the Egyptians carefully moved old temples. The lake that the dam created would have flooded the temples.

## Glossary

**barrier** (BARE ee er) — that which blocks the path or flow of something

**dike** (DIKE) — a wall or bank to control water

**hydroelectric** (hi dro eh LEK trik) — relating to electricity produced by water power

**mill** (MILL) — a building with machinery to grind grain; the machinery used to grind grain

**reservoir** (REH zer vor) — a human-made lake in which water is stored

**spillway** (SPILL way) — a passage for "extra" water to pass over or around a dam

# INDEX

beavers  5, 6
Dam, Aswan High  22
Dam, Grand Coulee  14
Dam, Grand Dixence  14
Dam, Itaipu  14
Dam, Nurek  22
Dam, Rogunsky  22
dams
  beaver  5
  concrete  5, 14
  costs of  19
  dirt  6, 11
  height of  5, 22
  length of  5
  outlets of  16
  parts of  16
  problems with  19
  stone  6
  uses of  9
dikes  11
Egypt  22

Egyptians  22
electricity  9, 20, 22
fish  19
floods  9
hydroelectric power  9, 19
Lake Mead  20
lakes  5, 9, 11, 16, 19
mills  9
ponds  5, 11, 16
reservoir  16, 19
River, Columbia  20
River, Colorado  20
River, Nile  22
River, Tennessee  20
rivers  11
spillway  16
Soviet Union  22
Switzerland  14
Tennessee Valley Authority  20
Washington  14
waterwheels  9